MW00962639

DEFINING MOMENTS IN CANADIAN HISTORY

THE BATTLE OF VIMY RIDGE

Weigl

Published by Weigl Educational Publishers Limited
6325 10th Street S.E.
Calgary, AB T2H 2Z9
Website: www.weigl.com

All of the Internet URLs given in the book were valid at the time of publication. However, due to the dynamic nature of the Internet, some addresses may have changed, or sites may have ceased to exist since publication. While the author and publisher regret any inconvenience this may cause readers, no responsibility for any such changes can be accepted by either the author or the publisher.

Library and Archives Canada Cataloguing-in-Publication Data available upon request.
Fax (403) 233-7769 WEIGL for the attention of the Publishing Records department.

ISBN 978-1-77071-615-5

Printed in the United States of America in North Mankato, Minnesota
1 2 3 4 5 6 7 8 9 0 14 13 12 11 10

072010
WEP230610

Project Coordinator: Heather C. Hudak
Author: Penny Dowdy
Editor: Bill Becker

We gratefully acknowledge the financial support of the Government of Canada through the Canada Book Fund for our publishing activities.

Contents

Overview

From 1914 to 1918, the major powers of the world fought in World War I. England, France, Russia, and, eventually, the United States fought against Germany and its supporters. Canada, as a colony of Great Britain, formed an army and sent it to work with the British troops. In April 1917, Canadian troops set out to take Vimy Ridge from German forces. French and British forces tried many times to force the Germans back from the ridge, but failed. The Canadian forces used new equipment and techniques to succeed where others failed.

Vimy Ridge is a hill above the French town of Arras. The ridge is 8 kilometres long and overlooks the entire area. From here, German troops could see all of the movements made by the French and British troops. This made attacking the Germans on the ridge very difficult. The Germans also built tunnels and bunkers, which gave them excellent protection during attack. At dawn on April 9, 1917, 35,000 Canadian troops attacked the ridge. After three days of heavy battle, the Canadians were victorious. The victory symbolized Canada's military strength.

Background Information

Julian Byng - Sir Julian Byng was a general in the British army during World War I. He led the Canadian troops in the Battle of Vimy Ridge. He later served as governor-general of Canada.

Arthur Currie - Sir Arthur Currie was a Canadian teacher, businessman, and soldier who joined the Canadian military. He was the first commander in the newly formed Canadian military, and he helped design the attack on Vimy Ridge.

Colour of uniform worn by each country during World War I

Canadian Army

French Army

British Army

German Army

GREAT BRITAIN DECLARED WAR ON GERMANY ON AUGUST 4, 1914, AND THE WAR QUICKLY BECAME KNOWN AS THE GREAT WAR. LATER, IT WAS CALLED WORLD WAR I. CANADIANS EAGERLY JOINED THE WAR TO ASSIST GREAT BRITAIN.
I WILL BE HONOURED TO SERVE IN THE CANADIAN CORPS, SIR.
TENS OF THOUSANDS OF CANADIANS AGREE WITH YOU. THE GERMANS WON'T STAND A CHANCE!

CANADIAN TROOPS TRAINED IN BOOT CAMPS IN GREAT BRITAIN.
WE GOT TO **BOOT CAMP** IN SEPTEMBER, AND NOW IT'S DECEMBER. I THOUGHT WE WOULD BE FIGHTING IN FRANCE BY NOW.
I HEARD THE GENERAL SAY WE WOULD BE TRAINING HERE THROUGH THE WINTER.

CANADIAN TROOPS PROVED THEIR BRAVERY AT THE SECOND BATTLE OF YPRÈS.
THAT'S CHLORINE GAS! THE GERMANS ARE POISONING THE FRENCH SOLDIERS!
WE CAN'T LET THE ENEMY TAKE THE FRENCH POSITION. MEN! SPREAD OUT, AND PUSH THOSE GERMANS BACK!
CANADIAN TROOPS WERE SOME OF THE FIRST TO USE TANKS IN BATTLE.
THIS TANK MOVES SLOWER THAN I HOPED. THE **ARTILLERY** IS PASSING US. AT LEAST THE TANK CAN ROLL OVER THE **BARBED WIRE** IN THE TRENCHES.

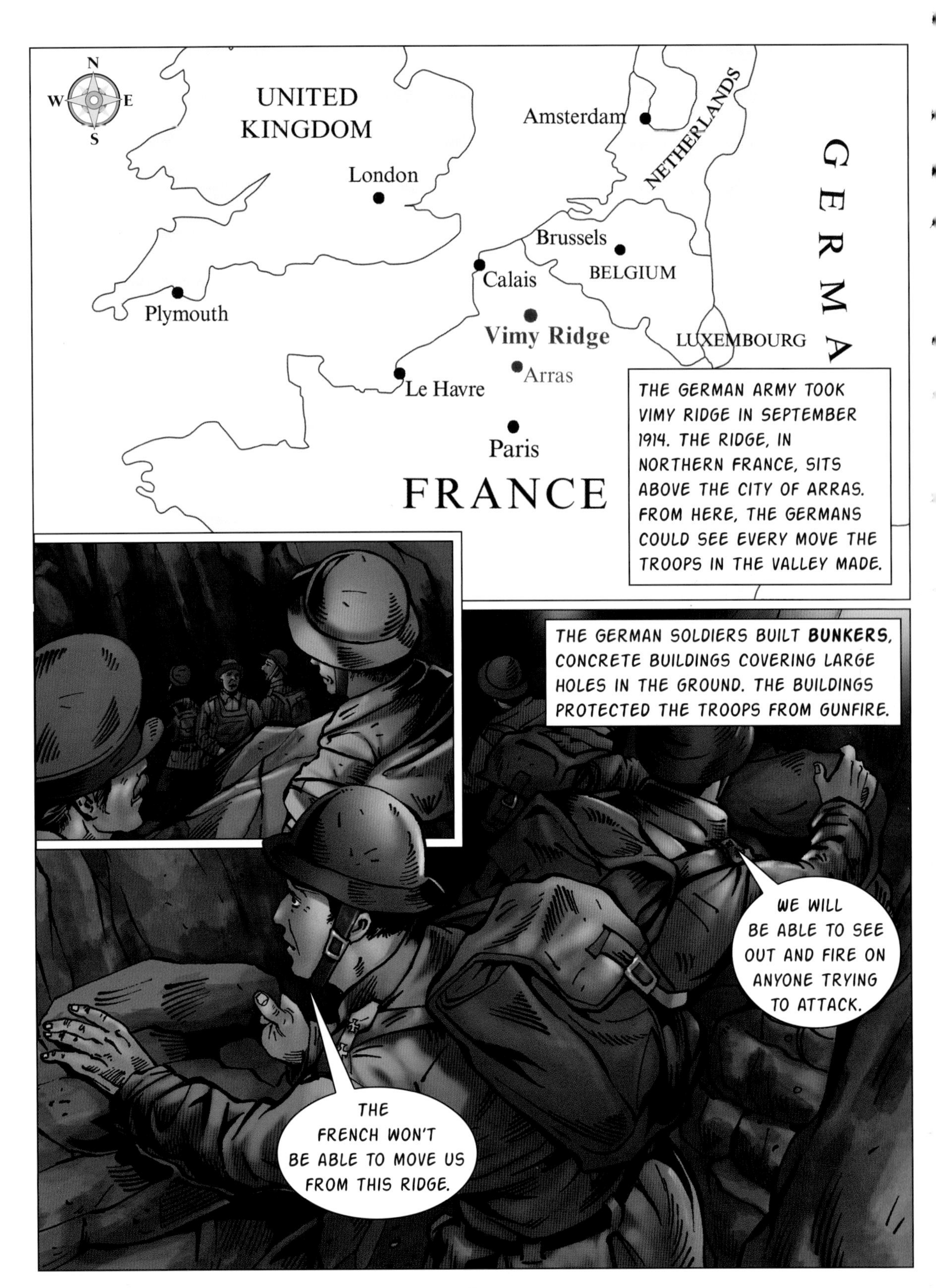
N
W
E
S
UNITED KINGDOM
Amsterdam
NETHERLANDS
GERMA
London
Brussels
BELGIUM
Calais
Plymouth
Vimy Ridge
LUXEMBOURG
Le Havre
Arras
Paris
FRANCE
THE GERMAN ARMY TOOK VIMY RIDGE IN SEPTEMBER 1914. THE RIDGE, IN NORTHERN FRANCE, SITS ABOVE THE CITY OF ARRAS. FROM HERE, THE GERMANS COULD SEE EVERY MOVE THE TROOPS IN THE VALLEY MADE.
THE GERMAN SOLDIERS BUILT **BUNKERS**, CONCRETE BUILDINGS COVERING LARGE HOLES IN THE GROUND. THE BUILDINGS PROTECTED THE TROOPS FROM GUNFIRE.
WE WILL BE ABLE TO SEE OUT AND FIRE ON ANYONE TRYING TO ATTACK.
THE FRENCH WON'T BE ABLE TO MOVE US FROM THIS RIDGE.

TROOPS COULD SIT BEHIND **ENCAMPMENTS** AND FIRE ON ANY SOLDIERS WHO TRIED TO COME UP THE RIDGE.

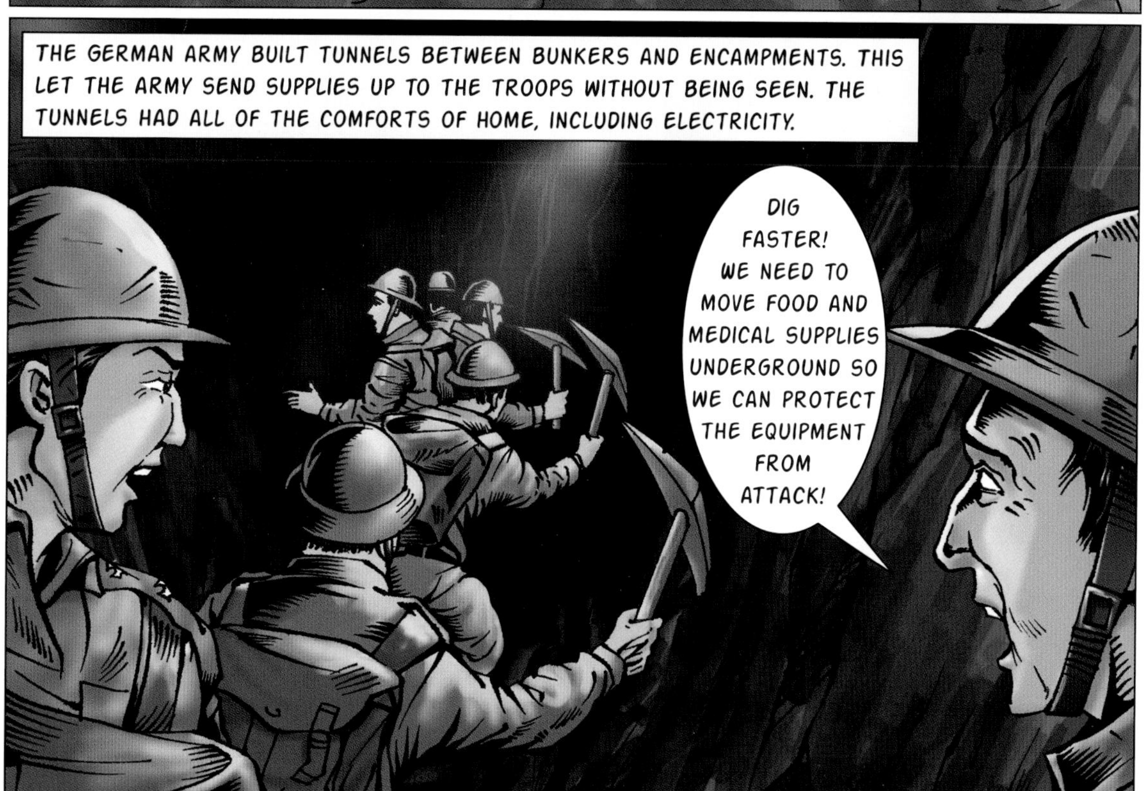
THE GERMAN ARMY BUILT TUNNELS BETWEEN BUNKERS AND ENCAMPMENTS. THIS LET THE ARMY SEND SUPPLIES UP TO THE TROOPS WITHOUT BEING SEEN. THE TUNNELS HAD ALL OF THE COMFORTS OF HOME, INCLUDING ELECTRICITY.
DIG FASTER! WE NEED TO MOVE FOOD AND MEDICAL SUPPLIES UNDERGROUND SO WE CAN PROTECT THE EQUIPMENT FROM ATTACK!

FROM VIMY RIDGE, THE GERMANS LAUNCHED DEVASTATING ATTACKS ON ARRAS. WAR CORRESPONDENTS FOLLOWED THE PROGRESS OF THE BATTLES. THEIR OBSERVATIONS WERE PRINTED IN NEWSPAPERS IN GREAT BRITAIN, CANADA, AND THE UNITED STATES.
THE GERMAN ATTACKS LEFT THE TOWN OF ARRAS IN RUBBLE. SOME HOMES, BUILDINGS, AND BUSINESSES STILL STAND, BUT MANY MORE ARE DAMAGED OR RUINED.

IN 1915, FRENCH SOLDIERS ATTEMPTED TO TAKE VIMY RIDGE.
LET'S SHOW THE FRENCH THAT TAKING BACK VIMY RIDGE WILL BE AN IMPOSSIBLE TASK!

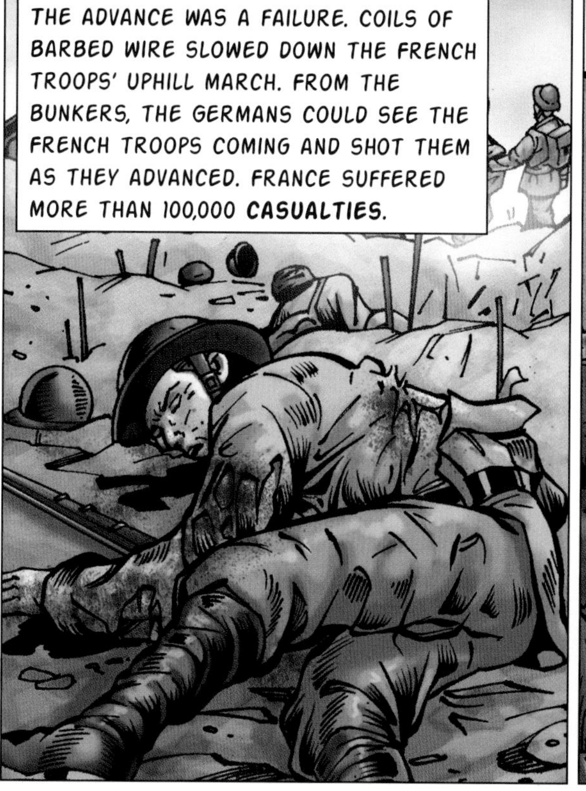
THE ADVANCE WAS A FAILURE. COILS OF BARBED WIRE SLOWED DOWN THE FRENCH TROOPS' UPHILL MARCH. FROM THE BUNKERS, THE GERMANS COULD SEE THE FRENCH TROOPS COMING AND SHOT THEM AS THEY ADVANCED. FRANCE SUFFERED MORE THAN 100,000 **CASUALTIES**.

BRITISH SOLDIERS TRIED TO PUSH THE GERMANS OFF THE RIDGE IN 1916. THEY FAILED. THE BATTLE CLAIMED BOTH BRITISH AND GERMAN CASUALTIES, BUT THE GERMAN **BATTLE LINES** HELD FIRM.
WE JUST CAN'T CATCH THEM OFF-GUARD. THEY CAN SEE US COMING FROM THEIR BUNKERS BEFORE WE EVEN GET CLOSE.

GENERAL JULIAN BYNG CAME TO FRANCE TO LEAD THE CANADIAN CORPS. THE CORPS HAD THE JOB OF SUCCEEDING WHERE OTHERS FAILED. THEY WERE TO CAPTURE VIMY RIDGE.
I KNOW YOU ARE AWARE THAT THE GERMANS HAVE BEEN IN CONTROL OF VIMY RIDGE SINCE 1914. I INTEND TO CHANGE THAT.

ARTHUR CURRIE LED ONE OF THE FOUR CANADIAN DIVISIONS UNDER BYNG. CURRIE WORKED WITH BYNG TO PLAN THE ATTACK ON VIMY RIDGE.
WE HAVE TO DO THINGS DIFFERENTLY IN ORDER TO DRIVE THE GERMANS OUT OF THE BUNKERS AND TUNNELS. ALL FOUR **DIVISIONS** OF CANADIAN TROOPS WILL BE INVOLVED IN THIS ATTACK.

CURRIE STUDIED THE FAILED ATTEMPTS TO TAKE THE RIDGE SO HE COULD UNDERSTAND WHAT WENT WRONG.
I SEE...ONCE YOUR COMMANDING OFFICER WAS INJURED, YOU DIDN'T KNOW WHAT YOU WERE SUPPOSED TO DO.

CURRIE AND BYNG DEVELOPED A DIFFERENT APPROACH TO FIGHTING THE GERMAN STRONGHOLD.
I HAVE QUITE A FEW IDEAS I WOULD LIKE TO SUGGEST, SIR. LET ME SHOW YOU.
THESE ARE OUTSTANDING IDEAS, CURRIE. THE GERMANS WILL NOT KNOW HOW TO DEAL WITH THIS TYPE OF ATTACK.

COMMANDING OFFICERS GAVE THE TROOPS AS MUCH INFORMATION AS POSSIBLE ABOUT THE UPCOMING BATTLE.
Vimy
VIMY RIDGE
GROUP VIMY
Arras
GROUP ARRAS
YOU SEE? THIS IS EXACTLY THE PATH WE WILL TAKE TO CATCH THE GERMANS BY SURPRISE.
THE ONLY THING WE DON'T KNOW IS WHEN WE ATTACK.

NEW TECHNIQUES, SUCH AS **AERIAL PHOTOGRAPHY**, HELPED BYNG AND CURRIE PLAN THE ATTACK. THE BALLOONS CARRIED CAMERAS THAT TOOK PHOTOGRAPHS OF THE GROUND BELOW. THE PHOTOS SHOWED THE CANADIAN LEADERS WHERE THE GERMAN SOLDIERS WERE HIDING.

THE TROOPS REHEARSED THE BATTLE SO THEY WOULD KNOW WHAT TO DO IF A COMMANDING OFFICER WAS INJURED OR KILLED.
IF THE CAPTAIN IS SHOT, WE JUST KEEP GOING. WE'VE ALL STUDIED THE MAP, SO WE KNOW EXACTLY WHERE TO GO, WITH OR WITHOUT THE CAPTAIN.
THE ATTACK WOULD BE VERY DANGEROUS FOR THE CANADIAN CORPS. MORE PEOPLE HAD DIED AT VIMY RIDGE THAN ANY OTHER BATTLEFIELD IN FRANCE.
I PRAY THAT OUR PLAN PREVENTS ANOTHER **MASSACRE** LIKE THE MEN BURIED HERE EXPERIENCED.

ALLIED TUNNELS WOULD ALLOW THE FORCES TO GET CLOSE TO THE GERMAN **FRONT LINES** BEFORE LAUNCHING THEIR ATTACK.

THEY WON'T KNOW WE ARE COMING UP THE RIDGE UNTIL IT'S TOO LATE!

THE GERMANS CAN'T SEE THE OPENINGS TO OUR TUNNELS BACK HERE.

SOLDIERS USED SCIENCE AND MATH TO CALCULATE HOW FAR AWAY GERMAN SOLDIERS WERE POSITIONED.
THAT FLASH MEANS THAT THE GUNNERS MUST BE 350 METRES AWAY.

A NEW KIND OF ARTILLERY SHELL WOULD EXPLODE WHEN IT HIT THE GROUND RATHER THAN DRIVE ITS WAY INTO THE EARTH BEFORE EXPLODING.
THESE SHELLS WILL BLOW AS SOON AS THEY HIT THE GROUND. THAT SHOULD DO MORE DAMAGE TO THE **TRENCHES** THAN OUR OLD SHELLS.

THE NEW ARTILLERY SHELLS WORKED. THE CANADIAN CORPS LAUNCHED ARTILLERY SHELLS FOR A WEEK BEFORE MOVING UP THE RIDGE, BADLY DAMAGING THE GERMAN FRONT LINES.

THE SURGE UP VIMY RIDGE STARTED ON EASTER MONDAY, 1917. AS THE TROOPS MOVED UP THE TUNNELS THEY BUILT, THE BELLS OF THE REMAINING CHURCHES **PEALED** THE EASTER MESSAGE.

SLOWLY, THE ARTILLERY MOVED UP THE RIDGE.
I DON'T SEE MANY GERMANS FIRING ON US.
I WONDER IF THEY ARE HIDING IN THE TUNNELS.

ARTILLERY AND TROOPS MOVED TOGETHER AT A SLOW AND STEADY SPEED UP THE RIDGE. THE TROOPS CALLED THIS THE "VIMY GLIDE." THE ARTILLERY COULD FIRE FIRST AND CAUSE MAJOR DAMAGE. THE TROOPS FIRED AT SOLDIERS THEY FOUND ALONG THE WAY.

ARTILLERY AND TROOPS MOVED TOWARD THE GERMAN FRONT LINES WITH A VICIOUS ATTACK.

THE WEEK'S WORTH OF ARTILLERY FIRE BEFORE THE SURGE UP THE RIDGE KEPT SOME OF THE GERMAN SOLDIERS FROM REACHING THEIR POSITIONS.

NOBODY'S HERE! WE'VE GOT 'EM ON THE RUN!

THE SURPRISE APPEARANCE OF THE CANADIAN TROOPS BEHIND THE ARTILLERY CAUGHT THE REMAINING GERMAN SOLDIERS OFF-GUARD.
YOU WON'T FORGET THE DAY THE CANADIAN CORPS CAME UP VIMY RIDGE.

THE ATTACK THAT BYNG AND CURRIE DEVELOPED WORKED EXACTLY AS PLANNED.
THE FIRST DIVISION HAS REACHED THE FRONT LINE! IT ONLY TOOK 30 MINUTES, SIR! THE FRONT LINE WILL BE OURS!

BY 6:30 A.M. EASTER MONDAY MORNING, MEMBERS OF THE CANADIAN CORPS WERE MOVING TO THE SECOND LINE.
DO YOU THINK WE'LL HAVE A FIGHT AT THE SECOND LINE?
I HOPE NOT! WE NEED TO KEEP FIRING ARTILLERY SHELLS AT THE MACHINE GUN ENCAMPMENTS SO THE GERMANS CAN'T GET TO THEM.

SOME GERMAN SOLDIERS DID NOT HAVE TIME TO REACH THEIR WEAPONS IN ORDER TO RETURN FIRE.
YOU THERE! GET ON THE GROUND. YOU ARE NOW A PRISONER OF WAR.

HOW'RE WE DOING?
IT'S GOOD, SIR. I THINK WE'LL WIN THIS ONE.

THE ATTACK KILLED MANY GERMANS. FEWER CANADIANS WERE INJURED OR KILLED THAN THE GERMANS.
WHAT IS IT, DOC?
IT'S JUST A FLESH WOUND. YOU'LL BE FINE.

BRITISH PLANES SEARCHED FOR GERMAN SOLDIERS HIGHER UP THE RIDGE.

THE CANADIAN ARTILLERY REACHED HIGH ENOUGH ON THE RIDGE TO SEE THE GERMANS MOVING SOLDIERS AND SUPPLIES UP THE RIDGE.
AIM FOR THE TRAIN! WE DON'T WANT THEM GETTING MORE GUNS OR **AMMUNITION**!

THE CANADIANS DESTROYED GERMAN BUNKERS. THE GERMANS HAD NOWHERE TO HIDE.
OVER THERE! LET'S GET THEM BEFORE THEY CAN REACH THEIR WEAPONS.
THIS WAS POSSIBLY ONE OF THE GREATEST VICTORIES I HAVE EVER SEEN. THE CANADIAN FORCES WERE SIMPLY BRILLIANT.
WITHIN THREE DAYS, THE ALLIED FORCES CONTROLLED VIMY RIDGE. MORE THAN 10,000 CANADIAN SOLDIERS WERE INJURED, AND 3,000 DIED. THE GERMANS SUFFERED ABOUT 20,000 CASUALTIES.

THE BATTLE OF VIMY RIDGE WAS THE MOST SUCCESSFUL ALLIED ATTACK IN THE REGION TO DATE.
GENERAL BYNG, I THINK WE HAVE WITNESSED HISTORY.
YES, CURRIE, YOUR CANADIAN MEN SHOULD BE VERY PROUD OF THEMSELVES.

THE BATTLE OF VIMY RIDGE SAW ALL FOUR CANADIAN DIVISIONS FIGHTING TOGETHER, WITH PEOPLE FROM ALL PARTS OF CANADA.
IT WAS LIKE WE HAD BEEN FIGHTING TOGETHER ALL ALONG.
OUR CANADIAN CORPS HAS COME A LONG, LONG WAY FROM THE FEW THOUSAND TROOPS WE HAD BEFORE THE WAR. NOW, WE ARE TENS OF THOUSANDS STRONG.
AFTER THEY HEAR ABOUT OUR VICTORY AT VIMY RIDGE, MORE MEN WILL CERTAINLY WANT TO JOIN US!

THE SUCCESS UNDER CURRIE'S LEADERSHIP AND WITH THE COORDINATION OF ALL FOUR DIVISIONS SHOWED THAT CANADA HAD THE MILITARY STRENGTH AND SKILL TO SUPPORT AND PROTECT ITSELF.
YOU SHOULD BE PROUD TO BE CANADIAN, CHILDREN. WE HAVE ONE OF THE STRONGEST ARMIES IN THE WORLD.
VICTORY OF CANADA

CANADIANS STOOD SEPARATE FROM GREAT BRITAIN.
"IN THOSE FEW MOMENTS, I WITNESSED THE BIRTH OF A NATION."

IN DECEMBER 1922, THE FRENCH GOVERNMENT GAVE THE CANADIAN GOVERNMENT 101 HECTARES OF LAND ON VIMY RIDGE ON WHICH TO BUILD A MONUMENT. DIGNITARIES FROM GREAT BRITAIN, FRANCE, AND CANADA UNVEILED THE COMPLETED **MEMORIAL** ON JULY 26, 1936. THE VIMY MEMORIAL HONOURS THOSE MEN WHO FOUGHT AND DIED TO HELP FORCE GERMANY OFF THE RIDGE.
SILENCE ET RESPECT
Accés interdit à tous vehicules roulant ainsi ouá tous les animaux., méme tenus en laisse
No vehicles no animals (even leashed) are allowed beyond this point

FRANCE OWES THE PEOPLE OF CANADA OUR DEEPEST THANKS. YOUR YOUNG MEN PUT THEIR LIVES ON THE LINE FOR THE FREEDOM OF OUR PEOPLE.
THE LAND STILL HAS ACTIVE MINES, SO PEOPLE ARE NOT ALLOWED ON CERTAIN PARTS OF THE GROUNDS AROUND THE MEMORIAL.
PEOPLE ARE NOT ALLOWED OVER THERE. SOMEONE COULD STEP ON AN OLD MINE AND SET OFF AN EXPLOSION.
MORE THAN 11,000 MAPLE TREES GROW ON THE GROUNDS NEAR THE MONUMENT. THE TREES WERE PLANTED TO HONOUR THE NUMBER OF CANADIAN SOLDIERS MISSING AFTER WORLD WAR I. THE SOLDIERS' NAMES ARE INSCRIBED ON THE MONUMENT.

Brain Teasers

1. Why was Vimy Ridge such a strategic location for the Germans?

2. How did barbed wire impact troop movement up Vimy Ridge?

3. How had the British army improved artillery shells?

4. Why did Byng and Currie have troops fire artillery shells for a week before they advanced on the ridge?

5. How did the Battle of Vimy Ridge help move Canada toward becoming an independent nation?

6. Why were tanks so important in this battle?

7. What do the maple trees at the Vimy Memorial commemorate?

Answers

1. The German soldiers could see the movements of enemy troops in the valley below.
2. It slowed troops on foot and tangled in the wheels of the artillery.
3. The shells now exploded when they hit the ground, rather than driving into the ground and then exploding.
4. The artillery shells damaged the barbed wire, bunkers, and machine gun encampments, so the troops on foot could move more easily and not be fired upon.
5. It showed Canadians, Great Britain, and the world that the Canadian military was strong enough to defend the people of Canada.
6. The tanks could travel over the barbed wire in the trenches without being damaged.
7. The trees represent the Canadian soldiers who were missing at the end of World War I.

Further Information

How can I find out more about the Battle of Vimy Ridge?

Most libraries have computers that connect to a database that contains information on books and articles about different subjects. You can input a key word and find material on the person, place, or thing you want to learn more about. The computer will provide you with a list of books in the library that contain information on the subject you searched for. Non-fiction books are arranged numerically, using their call number. Fiction books are organized alphabetically by the author's last name.

Books

Batten, Jack. *The War to End All Wars: the Story of World War I.* Toronto: Tundra, 2009.

Hayes, Clair W. *The Boy Allies with Haig in Flanders Or, The Fighting Canadians of Vimy Ridge.* New York: A.L. Burt, 2010.

Granfield, Linda. *Where Poppies Grow: a World War I Companion.* Toronto, ON: Stoddart, 2001.

Websites

www.warmuseum.ca
War Museum of Canada website

www.vac-acc.gc.ca
Veterans Affairs Canada website, with a link to memorials, including the Canadian National Vimy Memorial in France

Glossary

aerial photography: photographs of Earth taken from above its surface

allied: troops working with Great Britain and France

ammunition: bombs or bullets fired from guns

artillery: large firearms, such as cannons, that move on wheels

barbed wire: wire with sharp points of metal spaced evenly along it

battle lines: the lines where warring troops meet

boot camp: a camp where people who recently joined the military receive training

bunkers: shelters that are dug in the ground and reinforced for protection

casualties: military people injured or killed during warfare

divisions: large groups or parts of an organization

encampments: mounds of dirt or small cement walls that protect soldiers from attack

front lines: the first lines of soldiers where warring troops meet

massacre: a massive amount of killing

memorial: an object constructed in the memory of a person or event, especially a monument

pealed: rang bells loudly

trenches: ditches from which soldiers fought

Index